The Apothecary of Flight

The Apothecary of Flight

Jane Burn

Nine
Arches
Press

The Apothecary of Flight
Jane Burn

ISBN: 978-1-913437-96-1
eISBN: 978-1-913437-97-8

First published July 2024 by:

Nine Arches Press
Unit 14, Sir Frank Whittle Business Centre,
Great Central Way, Rugby.
CV21 3XH
United Kingdom

www.ninearchespress.com

Printed in the UK on recycled paper by Imprint Digital.

Nine Arches Press is supported using public funding by Arts Council England.

Supported using public funding by
ARTS COUNCIL
ENGLAND

Contents

"Hope" is the thing with feathers—
That perches in the soul—
And sings the tune without the words—
And never stops—at all—

– Emily Dickinson

The Apothecary of Flight

After 'Our sweetest songs are those that tell of saddest thought', Percy Bysshe Shelley

I am clearing the page of birds   Beneath the thought of feathers
            is a person who writes
                    I will do this
away from the apothecary of flight   and this next work will be
            a recantation of wings

I will ask *who are you, poet?*   *What if you could not write the sky?*
If all the shades of blue are denied?
I will strip away your weight   and guide you away
                    from your bones
You must not whisper   or mutter or skein   but stand
with your poem loud and like a beacon   in your hand
I see you   washing words in water
throwing yourself upon   the elucidation of the sea

        Is it possible to write yourself clean?   Refrain

from the solution of puddles   Step away from the stream
    (except a stream of consciousness)
I see you   peeping out between the trees! See how you run
    straight back to your   ornate autarky!

How do you see immortality?   Will you fall
and be devoured by the ground?   Are you the fate of leaves?
    Wear your sonnets like a crown   and leave the bosky
to the forest   *Our sweetest songs are those that tell*
of saddest thought   (how full doth that line make

thy plain heart feel!)   so name things (without shame things!)
    Say it strong

  Make them know that every day
                is a precipice
Taste instead the tongue's deliverance
Raise your voice   Speak the clarity of ice

This poem must be about

something of unbearable consequence   something massive, like
the abscission of daffodils   (in a green glass vase on a windowsill)
and the way they embody a matter of great importance   possibly
the sadness of the ageing process   beauty's brief skin   or
our inevitable deaths   otherwise
it runs the risk of being just another poem about flowers   Just
another poem about   their overwhelming scent   their dust

spent for no reason   impotent on the sill's embroidered cloth
The water's false hope of life everlasting   The unquenchable thirst
that their poor yellow heads will never understand   This must not be
just another poem about wilting   or confusion at the absence
of rain that they somehow still sense   their petals slanted
toward the day, politely asking for light   *My mother*
hated me, I tell them   They answer   *yes, my dear   we know*

An Imaginary Residency Inside an 18th Century Stoneware Jar

For the last month, this jar has been more than home. It has been
lonelier than I ever imagined but I have made a friend of echoes —
have lined this space with song. I must react and interact, inhabit
this vessel until it becomes my second skin. I wrote about durability,

longevity. How the outside is speckled like a tree sparrow's egg —
the pretty daubs of petal, crude and bold. I wrote about each change
to the circle of light, or dusk, or dark above my head. Sometimes,
the air cools to dew point and the glazed inside cries. It was odd

at first to see something so cold and hard weep but I think it best
to let it have its grief. Come within — for you may read, if you wish,
my ledger of scents. Being alone for so long has sharpened my sense
of this cavity's past, its bearing of oil, wine, water, vinegar, milk —

the people that have borne it in their arms, against their chests
like a heavy child. I smell their breath, for they have held their faces
above, like peculiar moons. I write in the language of kilns —
dunt and *fettling, greenware, sintering.* I have measured this place

for sound — for the trace of every voice that has echoed down.
The jar's body is ringed, in memory of the potter who raised it
on their wheel. Sometimes dizziness sets in. I have learned the peril
of corners — how they try to send you straight, how they attract

the shadows. I live without them happily now, forever in the round.
I must tend the hairline crack, threading from the base and feeding upon
an old weakness. The jar no longer rings true. It returns the noise
of faulty bone. You are welcome to join a workshop here but

take care; clay has a way of drawing impurities out. I am eager
for stories — the jar's destiny is to swallow whatever we give. Please
fill me with your words. I ask you all this same question,
after you climb in — *so tell me: what did you once hold?*

Too many dawns are grinding you down

Each of them fingered under the door, like a rankling note
from enemy hands; sly and meant to leave a bitter edge — time
today will wear all shapes of mean. Start and intend to go on. Start
by lapping at dirty words. Fail to speak in skylarks. The night
has never been enough. You do not savour morning as you should.
Shift your unreadiness — you must rise, unassembled and scarecrow
the mattress on broomstick bones; beware the sham of half-light clinging
round your bed. Raise your skin and flail its ballast of unkempt sleep.
You have been disrupted, fouled aware by a clock's meddling bleat.
Sometimes you have come. Sometimes you have cried—
you know this from the salt, scribbled upon your cheeks. The air still
claims *you have no kin. You are not loved.* These are the curses

that coil inside your unsuspecting head—
the breaths that you take from the dark.

When I was sent to Coventry for real

Coventry is a shithole, the posh bloke from up the road said.
My son will not be going to university there. I want to unpack everything
about his comment — it's a real onion of a thing to say.
There are so many layers of privilege, I don't know where to begin.
When I was sent to Coventry for real, everyone made that same joke.
What did you do to deserve that?
It's an unkind fate, to be cut from the herd —
to be marked with shame, to be shunned. Coventry
is one of the best places I have ever been.
So many excuses to stop, spend some moments in wonder.
In the Precinct, a poem is carved into rills — the water weaves
with words; history speaks from beneath its shallow shine.
Lady Godiva was sent to Coventry too. In Broadgate, she is skinned
with verdigris bronze, written into the signs of local shops.
In the '50s clock tower, she is chimed out every hour
from automatic doors. She says nothing.
I went out early so I could be alone with the Cathedral's stones.
In the bombed part, I cried for the broken blooms of glass that cling
the blitzed tracery like lozenges of multi-coloured fruit.
Just like this place, I thought that I was broken once — we are stories
of ruin yet built ourselves brand-new. How amazing
that the skeleton remains — its scars are truth and truth is
the most wonderful thing. Heaven is limitless. Prayers are birds
and snow, sun, stars, and sky. Its psalms were honest, rough, and wild.
I didn't go there for perfect — I did not mind the yellow hazard sign
in front of the Baptistery Window, nor the other folk wandering about.
This place told me its pain. The window wall of light is etched
with gorgeous ghosts. The tapestry's green is the Elysian Fields.
If this is Coventry, I thought, *then I'll stay.*
The silence here is beautiful.

Translation / Acts

Sperm and egg translate [sometimes] to flesh, wet womb to dry air,
water's peace to screams. Need translates to milk — to a gum's burden
of invading teeth / bone to longer bone,

dense to brittle. Night is traded for day,

sensations / perceptions of dark / interpretations of light — asleep
for awake, insomniac to agony, unconsciousness to consciousness,
fatigue to [maybe] less fatigue, [brief] solace

to overwhelming fear — prone to an image

of wings / of the risen Christ / prone to stay the fuck right here / need help.
Bladder empties out to shame / relief, thirst to slake [should there be supply],
sour breath to minty fresh — [if possible]

dirty to clean, hungry [if food exists] to fed,

energy to attempt, journey [in inches or miles] to arrival, travail
to frustration / pleasing ourselves / clocking in to [hopefully] some reward.
Deadlines become procrastination / achievement.

Skill turns to product / catastrophe. Potential

is fulfilled / morphs into waste, the future to futility / infamy / discovery /
erasure / regret. Laundry into angels pegged to a line / an undefeatable pile.
Time present submits to time past, and

years are rewritten / written off / unwritten.

You live / you hope / pain or fail — illness to illness / wellness to illness,
broken to fixed, fixed to broken, to more broken [plus all the shapes of health
between]. Love translates to loved in return /

loving [or not loving] oneself / unloved / to feeling

[being made to feel] unlovable / used to love [and don't, any longer]. Need
into compromise / intransigence, differences into solutions / a massive row.
Trust into confidence / faith / gaslighting /

      violence/ [in]security / doubt. Friend

to community / support / misunderstanding / loneliness. Hearts turn to stone,
grief to marrow, found to lost / rediscovered / Tears to tantrums / relief / futility.
Emotion to alexithymia. Masking to burnout. Throat to [uttered / imagined] howl,

      to air / fighting for air, to asking / silence / song.

Revelations   01/01/2022

try harder   lose weight   skim the plump from your clumsy bones
make a bit more of an effort   get fit   this is a new start   forget
the empty promises   grow your hair   vow yourself amazing

stop sleeping with people you only just met   stop making a danger
of your skin   stop taking risks   take more risks   do not think that
everything is broken   stop letting yourself slip through the cracks

become famous   be anonymous   earn money   manage the money
you earn   eat normally   be normal   fuck normal   learn to love Sundays
find love   you are not defined by love   tell people that mock your accent

how it makes you feel   tell yourself that you are equal   try to recognise
when you are doing something wrong   tell your value   moisturise
your feet   give up smoking   give up gin   discover what might be

bad for you   drink herbal tea   do fifty sit-ups per day   do twenty
sit-ups per   do ten   do five   aim for 10,000 steps a day   the Pennine
Way is about 250 miles   in six months you could walk from   learn

to wild camp   learn to drive by the age of 20   30   40   make sure
to pack a nutritious lunch   bake your adoration into cakes   cut down
on sugar   eat yourself well   try harder   go to the theatre   wear

comfortable shoes   walk on the beach   walk to the shops   take the
stairs   scarves are both functional and beautiful   you are beautiful
and functional   work hard   work harder   read   read better   write

write better   learn how to crochet   ask for help   ask for the right help
set the clock five minutes fast   learn to play the ukulele   de-clutter
write poems   write poems   smiles are the summer of the face   dispose

of every photograph that makes you feel ashamed   master your fear of
swallowing orange pith   imagine yourself as other   as hare   as horse
as deer   as whale   as bird   sing as though your child is listening

grow your own tomatoes   clear an hour each day for reading   notice
all the little things   learn the names of wildflowers   plant a tree   plant
another tree   find out who you are   find the story of your grandmother's

past   go back to school   repeat the word *academia* until it feels
comfortable in your mouth   endure the discipline of sonnets   always
carry a notebook   jot a few lines down every day   at least one word

Augury

After 'Prophétie' by Aimé Césaire

It's your quest. Your grail, your lucky rabbit's foot
            whatever you want to call it — life   Inside it, you will burn
        oh, so brightly. I see the flame, quiet as you are
                the end of your cigarette (if you are smoking)
against your lip like an exploding star Oh   *bite me!*   Come, come
and meet the others, speaking louder than the sun

all these women   radiant cheeks   spit those words
        from your brilliant throat — you spew luminance   woman
        gorgeous woman, phosphorescent thing!   Kiss me, it's fucking joyous
            See how you smell like a whole year of milk — backpaddle

over this pale sea or drown   die   whatever you think is best
        You're a goddam phoenix   and now the milk is ashes — scatter
each season away with one flick   of your great wings
        That shitty cellar where you grew so scared of dripping, leeching,
            dampstink things and dark   and the mould that grew on the wall
in the shape of Pentecost (because the door above was letting in tongues of light)
        When you thought that   GOD   was coming

straight for YOU   and got yourself mixed up in shades of HELL
        you trash, you apostolic babbler   crouched upon the floor
in droopy weeds, mourning all the shoes that used to fit   and all the while
you cried, a centipede loop-de-looped the ceiling
            with its 100 tincy feet   Oh yes, you're lush — remember that

you can leave anytime   Outside is night   rhubarb bleeds
        its squeaky-bony growing song   cabbage like a mirror of your own
        ageing face   There's a hive, somewhere   at the centre of the universe,
and its bees are made from spectacular gas   the honey they weave

is a sable welt of sky   Beneath, the knock of your heels on ground
         tap-tapping — this is the sound of you dancing   wonderful
     and completely out of time so pay no mind to despot clocks
       This notion of love — maybe on the dancefloor like *Electric Dreams*
          maybe   somewhere small and plain — cracks in a sidewalk,
     weak cement in a wall   Beware!   It flowers once in every twenty years
          in the hope of rain   But oh, not you —

you've seen it more than twice — I believe you might see it again Kiss me!
       Inside you, all those tastes of   pain   but always
    flavours of rainbow washing upon your clever smile   Woman,   you
         will inherit every castle you make with your head —
     your heart is its own prophecy   your tail streams the colour of smoke

    Oh, how you run along clifftops in defiance of the jaggy rocks below
    race to the edge of the ocean — you, melting   woman into the salt   Please,
        oh swiftling   spare your legs from a jackal's spite
            Your breast is wild horses   your air is wild horses —
            you are an island of horses

         your wild
           candescent skin   and
             your name

         shall be Wild Horses

when I balanced who I am upon the turning of a book

After *Tuesday*, by David Wiesner (as used in my NHS adult autism assessment)

on this page there are frogs frogs frogs
these have been the long waiting years   courage   have courage
you have been learning   who you are   you show the person
   your string   your soft blue handkerchief   your small spoon
so I had to look at all the pages from this book
     Tuesday   the book was called   *Tuesday*   and I said
clock   there's a clock   brightly lit up and the time says   almost nine
there are houses   seen from the roof   another doorway (also lit up)
trees   and on the next page (said the person doing the assessment)
what is happening   I said my head is very tired   I'm not a baby
     this seems more like a book for babies   I see grass
water   sky   trees with no leaves on them   probably winter or at least
cold   lily pads with frogs   a big moon   a turtle   night-time
lily pads with frogs on them and they are flying   silhouettes of birds
roosting on wires   I do my best to count the frogs   three frogs   four
     frogs and what looks like three crows flying
five frogs   frogs upside down   a tower with two bright dials
ten frogs flying on lily pads   white painted houses   the frogs
have big plain eyes   man at the table eating bread   milk   white
cupboards   table blender toaster yellow curtains   wall
clock says eleven twenty one   at the window flying on lily pads   frogs
fourteen frogs and bedsheets windows houses trees grass clothes line
I'm tired   let's keep going (said the person doing the assessment) frogs
frogs frogs (I think to myself   all fucking frogs)   in a fireplace   old lady
television seen from the back   wires lamp pictures wallpaper armchair
antimacassar glasses hair   what are the frogs doing (said the person
doing the assessment)   (heaven's sake) they are floating on (fucking)
lily pads same as all the other pictures   open doorway   cat   yellow dog
pink tongue frogs red brick chimney   frogs falling off hopping down
a country road going back in the water   three dogs police truck ambulance
blue sky   clouds man squatting   not long now (said the person doing
the assessment)   red barn wall   the shadow of a floating pig

weathercock   a wooden fence   (I'll be thinking frogs for the rest
        of my life)   a big dark roof   a heap of straw
well done (said the person doing the assessment)   I never thought
                that this is how
                    I'd be defined
I'd rather be made from all the little bits   of all the things I brought
        or read   or saw   I choose to be a wheel of time   a wheel of moon
        in the sky   the glassy gyre of a mild amphibian's eye
            the silver wheel of a spoon's back
            I choose to be   blue
                    I choose to be
                    myself

The National Trust Cannot Charge You To Come In

After Cottage No. 9, Ferry Landings, built 1919

Beneath our small wooden home, I found a web of snares.
This house, raised above the damp ground, once held
a coney web of easy meat. Half-captured by the soil,
twists of old wire lay crimped like a Sutton Hoo torc.
This is what I dig — a worthless record of itinerant folk
who buried food beneath to keep it cool — this common people
archaeology, this archiving of undocumented life.
There was a human hand around the body of this soda bottle,
a child's mouth around a neck of vanished milk.
No list of names, just a knowledge of people trying to live,
as far as you can know them in the colours of the walls,
the years of soot weighing the roof beams, the ghosts
of gaslight making dirty moons on each mismatched ceiling —
buckled, cluttered with somebody else's mistakes.
With duty of care, I peel away the layers of age —
each threadbare skin of linoleum wearing the tracks
of anonymous feet — down under 1930's speckled-egg green,
are leaves of newspaper. Tawny and frail with age,
they suffer the name of Hitler — his being made chancellor
said as if it was just an everyday thing. No wonder
they are the colour of buried bones. The clay-heavy garden
is seeded with pieces of so many plates, as if to grow
another means to hold their meals, as if to grow above
as porcelain blooms — hints of blue, red, pink and painted flowers—
write about something you know, they always say,
and I know how important it is to fill your home with cheap
but precious things. See this bit of cup handle, bent
like a small creature's rib. See how there is the shape
of a finger nestled there still. I found a homemade cricket bat,
wormy with holes, the handle bound with rags and it broke
my heart. A flyblown mirror that holds no face (you will work,
you will disappear), pans, burned from the bottom
and folded shut — a bike, buried like the skeleton of a horse.

More snares — a history of stolen throats — an empty tin
of lead shot, an ossuary of long-toothed skulls, old pennies,
round and dead and dull, their figures haggled smooth,
the copper ready to answer with shine the least of tender rubs,
like new blood. Buttons, needles. Here I find all their useful bits.
Each wing of wallpaper I pull away is a narrative of choice
and hope, a claiming of bright — the yellow sun of a saucer —
my home is made from stories, all untitled, and until I came here
with my need to seek them, lost.

Epiphany / Turning 50

Whoever said there is a time and a place for everything
never heard you sing. Clocks are a curious breed.
Admire their charming faces — don't fall for their finger-pointing,

tick-tock idiolect. When they stop, respect their silent creed.
Shun the rudeness of alarms. Accept that it is morning because of birds.
Make time to hear their songs. Take your own sweet time.

Breathe in. Breathe out. Be wary of those who preach the gospel
of seizing days, who warn you that time is marching on.
Take the scenic route past the church or canal. Give everyone the time

they deserve. Time is not money. Hire a rowing boat indefinitely —
nobody will ever say *come in number 6, your time is up*.
Come when you're ready. Go when you've had enough.

There will be a train at some point. Three trains at once. Buses
are a law unto themselves. Treat life as a quest. You're the hero
who made it home. Surprise yourself with a dandelion gone to seed.

Look askance at notions of lunch. Forget to make soup.
Noon is a four-letter word in a stranger's mouth. Judge a loaf
by your nose — learn to trust your own skill. Guess your stomach

by changes of light. Supper will never be a loneliness of toast. Discover
peace when you stop killing time. Stop time in its tracks. Go to the beach
and be reminded how time and tide wait for no-one. Make up for lost time.

Stay out much too late. Who is midnight anyway? How often were you told
time is a healer? Accept that time has made a mockery of your waist. Read
a bedtime story when you feel most awake. Count blessings, not sheep.

Bear   i   Bear Bear Bear

has built her nest of things. She's practising being okay
for this Age of Staying In. She's sluggish with fear —
pulls the room around her tight and grizzles the window,
bumps her snout to leave strangers the shape of a kiss on the glass.
She mutters at the loury sky, flops the slack gutter of her damp lower lip.
If it wasn't for the changing light, she might never guess the time of day.
She suspects the clock of telling the hours in lies. Once, she was solitary
by choice. Sometimes she is busyness itself. Some nights lies awake,
listening to owls break the hearts of their prey. *Bear Bear Bear*.
If she doesn't repeat it, how will she remember her own name?
She's an odd bit, clutter of bones beneath her slovenly coat, clumped
where she can't be bothered to brush. She shores up her weight,
sways her wrecked hull from cupboard to plate. Everything tastes of boredom,
cheap bread and steel from her teeth on the fork.
She looks in the mirror and tongues salt from her dull claws.
Her gaze is petulant with bags. Her dewlaps beyond control.
There are many pictures on the walls. Her oil-on-canvas roses
with its car-boot nicotine smell. The junk-shop Jesus, turned
to face some distant pain. Boredom makes her do the daftest things.
She has taken His image down, played noughts and crosses in the dust,
stuck on googly eyes, prayed and cursed. It never made one jot of difference
to the endless weeks. He told her *the state of your life is not my fault.*
She said *do you even like bears?* Through this sad hibernation, she craves
the taste of air. She owns a cottage suite, pelted with crochet throws,
too tiny for her frame. *How do?* says Bear. She talks to imaginary friends
or sits inert for hours, listening to the rain. One day she'll shoulder the door
of her den. Walk and not feel the loneliness of the streets, not feel
as if she must make a muted hoard of her own breath. She'll smile,
peel the mask from her beaming. She'll find someone to hug.
She'll sing the rust from her voice.

On Hawkburn Head

Nothing but moor and me for miles. Sometimes it's good to want
to be lost. Truth is, I'm as found as I ever was — at the car park
a sign pins me to the ground (Lydgett's Junction, 6.6 miles / You
are here) — so I pretend a sense of mystery, pass from the sight

of the main road and I could be anything. Could stand here forever,
counting the tastes on my breath — the acres go to the bottom
of my lungs. I savour hints of burrow, flight, mist and track,
stone and peat, swallow the scents in deep then sigh

the wildness out. Here is a history of bloom — bog asphodel,
melancholy thistle, false sedge — their names are alive in my mouth.
Seeds are patient ghosts, waiting to be remade beneath
the season's resting skin. The landscape yields in subtle rolls

as I aim for the reservoir, its silver wound skinned with clouds.
Wind cuts the water into serulate shapes. I didn't realise
how dull, how stale, how loose, how soft, how blunt I had become
until I came to this place. I crouch in the aisle

of an old rut and sense the soil's song as it raises crowns of rush.
There's a faraway house, tucked in a fold — its windows must shrine
with coins of evening sun. It's cold but there is a bright blue sky
above the burnt heather, the lime-green moss. On an outcrop,

wary Swaledales turn their smit-marked backs.
Grouse scrape the air. I am not lonely here, though I am alone.
Puffballs blink a smoke of spores. I see one bleached femur,
swabs of fleece, glossy milkcap tongues.

They tell you to come here to gaze at the dark — I imagine the night
speaking in stars, holding its chorus of faraway light. I owe this land.
This is my wayleave — my voice. The dreams I have.
The care I take with my feet.

Natural Occurrence (Driving Home from The Lakes)

Your hair Your waistcoat
the fells said *look* *this is the wrong time*

  to fall in love it's always the wrong time
  to fall in love I walked I slept I thought

 I was driving home on a steep road
 the sky will always take me away from You

the rain obscures each hill I cannot name
if I touched You I would crush You

  the fells said *there is only stone* *there is nothing else*
  love is five-hundred million years old

the fells were once an ocean they are salt You are salt
I am salt my heart is a mountain *there is only mountain time*

  the sky will take me back to where you are
  Your hands Your neck Your shoes

Aisling to Dún a Rí

I dreamed the forest away. Around me, a scalped horizon —
rain had nowhere to hang its gems. Sun cut the soil
with its bright knife. The well dried — each coin dull,

each wish denied. The Cabra River flayed its bare snake.
Rabbit's Bridge arched its poor bone across. I dreamed
of stumps, chainsaws and dust. I woke beneath an oak's

sweet shade, let birds sing the sadness from my mind.
Humus left damp moons on my knees.
The trees were real again, casting out their rippled shapes.

I saw where a mast year acorn had taken root —
claimed its part in the understory layer,
begun its desire for the sky.

Here is proof of new wood. Oh nascent oak! How lucky
that you grew here, exactly where I needed you to be.

At High Force

I wait for a different way of being.   Here, I will know the dark
and not be afraid. Here is void   and brightness, obscurity
and illumination settled side by   side. The rocks press against
absolute night. So many stars I   cannot divine. So many shapes
of heaven, half recognised, like   pages from a book come to life.
Everything is written. The   spangled chart of the dark heights,
the map that brought me here —   through Pennines heather,
Alston, Garrigill, on past Ashgill   Force's spilling threads —
the signed path to High Force. A   far-flying bird wheels;
what bird, I cannot tell. Ring ouzel   or merlin, perhaps;
a name with an inkling of old magic.   The trees crack and wisp,
shudder, shade and reach. Nothing is   completely obsolete —
bough and crown have songs of their   own. The moon
licks them luminous. Steady, I pick   my way across the stones
broken sharp along the bank. The   waterfall mists and roars,
moil and foam, rust and yellow   tinged. My reflection
clots the pool. I thought I knew   this person staring back
at me — this person made from   streams. Like a dog looking
into a mirror, I see only another   of my ilk, and not
my real self. *Nice to meet you,*   I say. *The pleasure's all mine,*
the face politely claims. I smash   my hand right through
its cheeks, lips, forehead, eyes.   My cuff is soaked.
I'm crying and I don't know why.   *I forgive you this savage act,*
the face looking up at me smiles,   *for people sometimes hurt*
what they do not understand. The   waterfall meets the edge
of the universe. All is nebulous.   I tilt my head.
There is another world. Up there,   above,
   above, above.

The Effects of Rage

After Storm Arwen, 26/27th November, 2021

Arwen came / pain between her teeth
   her name enough / to make the sound
of wrath / against this broken land /
       she told herself to us / in ways of massive ire
   we feared at the windows / like crated pigs
  afraid of whipcrack wire
      here is Bible / ! / says I /   *Armageddon* /
  brought on the tongue / of a storm
air became the shape / of knives / the shape
    of lump hammering /   *cruel* / *with fury*
   much will fall / before her squall's sight
bough and trunk / a puny tinder of boundary gate
     trampolines orbiting estates /   their lost moons / curious
upon a stranger's churned lawn / birds flayed from the sky
  rage / *rage against the dying of the light* / I threw her some words
    how else might one placate / such a rampant beast / ? /
     she ate the sound of poetry /   from the keen screech
of my own voice / gored my skin / with hurtled ice
  goaded the night / with thorny crowns of snow
come with your worst /   *hooligan*   / I shout my own waste
  against her / match her in this moment / crazed and wild
    my eyes / *my shoes* / *my rage* /
hold onto my house / claim it from her screaming fist
she is gnawing at the gable end /   *we're not in Kansas anymore*
     I defy this / scission / of her vicious breath
      defy her need / to break what I have built

where tulips fade and tongues are put to rest

After 'Tulips' and 'Edge' by Sylvia Plath

one brute sun   one linen moon   each claim a share of light
    slant across her mark   shape the hours from shadows
her plot   rewilds   resists   scree and sharp made anodyne
    by moss   becomes a sacred henge   her name held
in simple script   weather breaks against her slab   scalds or soaks
    the gifts of bloom   that glut its marl flank   and wish
their hale flush away   the faithful tread their pilgrimage   scrape pain
    into letters   pay her altar in coins or rocks   so we might prove
that we came   *Sylvia*   her name leans its myth upon our lips
    we sow a crop of plastic pens nib down into the soil   as if
to swell her place with ink   an oblation of poems aching
    to be said   the stems wait to fruit with words
while Celandine   Speedwell   and Campion thrive
    softly at her bed   wind sifts the Yorkshire fog
supple as a cat   subtle as breath   swallows pass on paper air
    take their communion with the sky   claim its wide peace
a weight of loam burdens   her seclusion   her hushed heart
    I tell her that I am lonely
    that everything here   is fear or drowning   I feel my family
against me like a scar   love cannot riddle   the taste
    of winter inside my head   we have hemmed her tomb
threadbare with our feet   as if to walk her back to life
    we kneel and try   to learn her through her work   adore
her ghost   the land remains awake   above this yard of bones
    nests frame pebble eggs   bees wear pillows of pollen's gold
roots bind the gentle dead   as seasons pass from bare to bloom
    the ground keeps its cargo of   cold   still   stones
the miracle of worms   beneath the snow's pure pall   a single rose
    is wasted there   stripped of thorns   pale as skin   closed

Mother Crow, Mother Bee, Mother Stone, Mother Sky, Mother Tree

I had a mother once   I called her *Crow*   for the way she perched
    her voice upon her tongue   *Crow* for the way her songs
    seemed full of early morning pain   *Crow* for her oil-shine curls
    for words shaped like a hollow frame   for claws

I called her *Bee*   for the way she worked her garden, knee-deep
in flowers, plucking out dead faces   *Bee* for every sting   *Bee*
  for the thought of honey in the stoppered tomb   of her heart
    I looked at my mother   at how she stood

as if each bone must accept the burden   of the other bone above
    I called her *Stone*   for the way her throat was a cold church
 Stone for the skinned hill of each clavicle, *Stone*   for the slab
    of her sleeping back, forever turned against

I called her *Sky*   for the way she hung her weight over my head
Sky for the shadow, blue from eyelid to brow   *Sky*
for the way she believed in angels   I remember how her lips
were like the edges of a broken cup   I felt how much

    she did not want to be touched   She said   *you children*
will be the death of me   *I had a daughter once* she said
    I called her Sea   *Daughter made from storm and salt*
      Sea for sickness, for drowning

  I threw her my love   it rattled like a pebble down a well
    I had a daughter once   she said *I called her Wrong*
for the way she was not thin or good   *Wrong for the way*
she was made   *Daughter*   *built from accidents*

I had a mother once   I called her *Tree*   for the way I hung
    from her arm like a leaf   the way I was shaken lose   *Tree*
  for the way I fell at her feet   *Tree* for the length of the shadow
    she cast   for the sun she tried to carry upon her crown

Rose, Redacted

After 'Les Roses', numbers i, viii & ix, by Rainer Maria Rilke

You dreamed yourself fat and rich with silk. Innumerable folds — O this weight of a bloated rose — shall I strip away your name? Your fate then shall be to roam our poems incognito. O rose, rose, another name, another sweet; crave and know the cruelty of thorns, you sickly thing — rose you could be love's antithesis, for all I know. You could be anything. How we must bundle you as passion's proof! A week's wage for a bunch of red — for a clot of one hundred severed heads! Rose, all such devotions of you will sit upon windowsills and wilt — will die one hundred deaths over the passing of a few ardent days. I have this picture of you, rose, bent over the morning sink, face made unearthly with tears, obedient to the weight of your massive, swollen head. The vase holds a funeral. What a strange and terrible gift you are, rose — even in your pastel coat, you bruise the colour of old flesh. Your bloom is divinely human, Saint Rose! Your bones must be allowed their beauty, though your barbs hook for blood — as if you must stitch yourself forever to some admirer's hand — your bud's knot will shuck, plump and vulval, heady, wondrous, splayed. You open out a scented shroud, attar against my naked skin like the first gown on a shamed Eve. Rose, my lover brought you to me, symbol of apology, obsession, hope and blatant need.

Taraxacum

I used to think it was because their yellow heads were manes.
Dandy little lions, I said. Free and nodding. I remember
how my guinea pigs used to squeak when I brought them
a handful I had picked. Their little eyes, their quickly crunching
teeth. K, A, C and E are their vitamins. Potassium, iron and zinc.
I found out it was the leaves — *dents de lion* — shaped like the bite
of a big cat's mouth. *Pissenlit, cankerwort, yellow gowan.* Inside
their stems, bitter milk. We have hauled them out, drowned
their hopes in glyphosate, expelled them from our squares
of sterile grass. The ultimate weed — pluck one head and it grows
another, mow it down, it comes right back, as if nature itself
is trying to tell us *Stop. Please stop.* They have nourished us
for centuries. Rinse the *radikia*, briefly boil, drizzle with lemon
and oil. Make tea. Hecate fed them to Theseus for thirty days
before he fought the Minotaur. Press the pappus against your lips
and breathe a wish. Blow and count the hours. Praise their defiance
of human harm, their reclamation of waste, their ruderality —
there are always cracks in concrete, no matter how small, room
for persistent roots, for bright faces, for determined greens.
They bloom wherever we break the land. I have a favourite
time and place — each summer, one side of a field where I live
becomes a gilded sea, pillow soft, filled to the brim with flowers,
kinetic with butterflies, bees and beetles dusted and drunk.
Bullfinch, linnet, sparrow, grouse and quail make a meal
of their seeds. Just one, set into a lawn as if it was the sun,
or the moon. A constellation, wheeling on the wind.

An Evanescent Garden

After *Horse's Skull with Pink Rose* by Georgia O'Keeffe, 1931

This bone has become an Eden. Picked clean
of unnecessary flesh, it is spared the tangling of thought,
the seeing of what cannot be unseen. Petals flush
upon its hollow skull — settle above its vanished life,
soften its truth with gentle bloom. Perfume fills the barren cave —
attar where eyes once turned like patient wheels,
marrow of scent replacing scarlet cells. And yet,

the head is plucked and without root, cannot keep its perfect skin,
will parch and dwindle, wither like a dead mare's pelt.
The forehead, smooth as a psalter's page is wreathed
by wings of green. The horse has forgotten its glorious self.
Instead of memory, an oubliette.
Instead of worry, light.
Instead of knowledge, air.

Ocular Map   Life as a Series of Roses

I am looking   empathy is   a useful thing
everywhere for roses   turning over stones
I am learning   making a collage   I spent a long time
how to reach the truth   of everything in my head   working out
    how to speak   once I did not see   the meaning of the word
once I saw   the distance   dialectics
all the somethings   only the foreground   I saw the bird
    not enough   of the nothings   but not the sky
        deep sea   true weather   what dialogue do I have

                                                with the past
    I look at shapes
        and I read   once in a while   light upon the page
        I saw myself   something catches my eye   as if I am
    as only a dress   an overflow of cold   still alive
        empty of body   steel skin   one by one
    the dirty water   had made a liquid of   I made a flood
    had scummed away   my laugh   of all the people
    my bones   a salt shell   I used to love

wholeness is   mostly I am
roses   useful as furniture
they provide escape routes   the suggestion
    imagine life as a series of roses   of missing pieces
    a geometry of painful things   a joyous tumble
        all of me coming out   being exactly where
        all my shapes   it needs to be
            I have written myself   unburdened
            unequivocal
        I am singing   I am roses
            I can love you
                I am

                free

The Bones and the Sky

The sterile path is not yet cushioned with new green.
It has become a mile of skeletons.
Along its edge, I see what is left of winter's death,
see where rabbits have left behind the truth of their bones,
how their frail kists of rib have fallen in,
how tooth and tongue have loosened their language to the soil.
I see the ruins of a crow — the bare keel of its breast,
the clavicle's unanswered wish. The wind fools its feathers into life —
I step over its weeds and think of you. I think about breath,
spent across the frost-bleached grass. I remember you laughing,
wide and wolfish and glad. Laughter, I pretend, is a living thing.
There is nourishment in the sound — where it falls, new roots grow.
See how they begin beneath old skin, push above the wastes of hair.
This seedling is the last time you smiled. The ground is full of you.
The earth took everything. Every time you cried,
it became part of the larger sky, like prayer.
We have gone from love to nothing.
I look at the clouds, grey in a dull sky. If I told you all the things
I do to make you stay, you'd roll your eyes.
You'd shake your practical head.
I keep your perfume by the bed and test my nose to our intimacies.
If I waste its precious mist, you come back to me as rain.
I nurse what is left of your sweat. I never washed that T-shirt —
a Eucharist of pheromones — the bread of your body,
the wine of your smell lie bunched in my arms like a cruel rose.
I place the tomb of your shoes on the mat as if you just said *hello*,
came in through the door. The air is so very beautiful
when I think of it on your mouth. I wonder if the birds above me know
how sweet they sound, or how high they seem.

The Women who are Dead

Each of the times that I have been   alive   each of the women
that swung upon my bones   each age   each clumsy bloom
is kept beneath the barrow of my skin   for there must be a place
to hallow what is left   I made my heart   into a charnel house

the women who are dead will always need   a place to still
their used and shacky selves   I laid these moon-faced hulls
into their own quiet shaft   the kinds of me that there has been
made a keepsake of   each ounce of blood   each different limb

Baby/me   quiet inside her wicker crib   little bloom of flesh
a cloistered gem   a cradle's cap of euphoric smell   Baby/me   knew
only small needs of milk and sleep   lengthenings of arm and foot
expansions of mouth and eye   ideas of face and light

Childhood/me offered to the catacombs of school   inchoate
against the playground's bruise   haunted by the warped home
of someone else's clothes   flailed at grammar's daunting plagues
Childhood/me   learned the shame of manifold tongues

Daughter/me   was not the right child   not good as gold
her name a hex   a strange bird vent from the cree
of her own mother's lips   Daughter/me   a bad gift
scratched at the walls of her changeling self

Vitiated/me   mouthed like sin through a confessor's grille
witness to a transgression of spires   the truculence of hands
the vile of milt and iron   debitage upon the puckered bed
Vitiated/me   shaped into grief

Wedded/me   tulle ghost led along an artery of stones
curing peevish days with pliant smiles   maundering at cupboards
raking a drawer's noise of forks   Wedded/me   peon
to a wall's pool of unrelenting time   had a throat of pearls

Mother/me   resting palms upon a crucible womb   afflictions
of slack and brindled skin   brooking every livid welt of pain
the glad insomnolence   Mother/me   curator of deciduous teeth
discovering   the sweet knife of a young spine

The Unknown Women

14th Century, Hexham Abbey

God be in my head, and in my understanding;
>   Be in our cobble heads   We understand the slow brutality
>   of time   Our weathering
>   our poor pebble shapes

God be in my eyes, and in my looking
>   Our eyes unmade   Faith be in the way we used to look
>   before our bodies were lost
>   God be in the crumbling
>   of chiseled sight

Faith be this obliteration   We cannot remember
>   You   We cannot remember ourselves

God be in my mouth, and in my speaking
>   Our voices are dust
>   canticles of ash dropped from a shovel
>   to the ground   The stain of soil

God be in my heart, and in my thinking
>   Our hearts are stone
>   God be in the skin   the mouth   the mind
>   our silence   our obscurity   our penitence

God be at my end, and at my departing
>   Each year has returned   another mote of us to the earth
>   Once there must have been words
>   in flight around us   Attrition has taken
>   our songs   our tongues carry no sound
>   Once   we recognised the taste of rain

God be at the erosion of our hands   the erasure of our names
>   How many acres of sky   have pressed upon our bones?
>   Were we anchorites?   Were we kind?

What have the centuries done
>   with womb and lung   rib   tooth   spine?
>   Did we marry?   Did we do what was expected of us
>   when we were still made
>   marrow-fresh   blood-red   luminous?

Going To Town With An Imaginary Friend

After 'The Panther' by Rainer Maria Rilke

Look how my clothes on the bed   make beautiful ghosts
    Don't wear that   she said · *or that or that or that*
it's me inside that spoils them   dressing all the time like a clown

paint like the apology of mummers on my face   She said *I know*
the courage it takes   Me   half an hour early for the bus for fear
        of lost opportunities   Sun passing through the shelter's seat

    writes a cage of shadows at my feet   It's too hot
I'm sweating now   She said   *don't you just hate that*
Gripping this great big bag   against my breast as if it was a found child

    She said *the middle of you is missing   You look like a stanza break*
in some poem about pain   It's this endless bearing
of unnecessary things   in case of rain or cold or thirst *it drags you down*

    she said   It weighs   at the space where my heart used to be
I have bothered it dry   with numerous affections   like a river
        that no longer gets enough rain   or a font that blessed

too many heads   She says   *you are always slightly tilted*
a tree that grows somewhere lonely   leaning against the wind
Subtle a a brick   you are   she said   I really wish

I was nine parts finesse and only   one part shame *try and be cool*
    try to raincheck the yabbering   She said *of course*
everybody left you behind   why would they want to walk

    beside your malarkey
        Inside me   somewhere   there is quiet
        I am all the subtleties

I just don't know
how to tell them that I am   She said
    they won't see   just as they would probably miss

        a bird's small death
            underneath the snow

43

I was a woman today

and I am not afraid of weather   not afraid of the hoar
scalding early cowslips   not afraid of brisking air
I shuck the pillows from their catchpenny shams   tawdry-bright
peg them   baggy with vaults of biting wind *rise your bellies*
bloat with painted flowers   fly   my chintz-beloved ghosts

and I am not afraid of dust have walked upon a Galilee of lint
like a saviour of filth   I am not afraid of the stove's ash   I rid it
using flags of sudsy cloth   here are the kitchen miracles
the hob roars with valiant stew *welcome*
to my church of scraped potatoes   spoon and eat

and I am not afraid of swans so lucky against my tired docility
filling their throats with elevated light   with an epiphany of air
I hear the peal of monumental wings   watch their passing over
of my tethered home   see them earn the clemency of sky
O send thy softly breasts to bright rivers   amen   amen

and I am not afraid of time   not afraid of the dial's divided eye
I see myself through years of perished skin   through its slackening
I grew a child   and despair of clothes around my drooping womb
the years blot my face and grope around my smile
take my pity of hands and salve their crackled plight

and I am not afraid of what I write   though the paper shrieks
beneath my raging pen   though I must empty my head of flames
of a long story of blood   of my own uneasy slipshod tell of truth
I offer all my burdens to this book   and scribble rivers
I love you   here are the umpteen many words I have for pain

At The Laing

I read this great little note about Synthetism at the side of
    The Breton Shepherdess and I thought   yes, completely yes,
        I would absolutely be a Synthetist
because I can't remember my third dimension

In front of *Isabella and the Pot of Basil* I realise that I don't
    have the profile to be a Pre-Raphaelite, or the figure or the hair
    I pause before *Jason in Hyde Park*   for ages
      I believe I can feel that sun on my neck
I can hear the distant birds, the bees, the underwater sounds
        of a soporific day
I am caught between all the pictures I would paint
    if only I had the inclination
       the courage, the ability,   the time

There are three young women in the gift shop buying cards
    that they will probably send to one another when term is done
       and they are home for the holidays
How solicitous they are to one another   how they clutch on
        as if one of them, at a moment's notice, might blow away
I watch them as one might watch butterflies
    I love them and they will never know that I do

A daughter meets her mother, getting off the bus
    how easily they fall into step
    how eagerly they smile

The moon is famous for its solitary form

The sun goes down alone
    and doesn't seem to mind

To sonnets and my best friend / horse

Just like this form, you hear no waste — ears turned
to flight or fear, or just my voice. Only necessary stuff
will fill your brain. The bigger the subject the better the smell,
you think — I see you roll your slovenly lip against
another horse's stool, the scent of rain, the sack of barley.
My body echoes in your head — how you taste me happy
or sad is a brilliant thing. You know me through your
manipulative tongue, test me with your cemetery of teeth,
then walk away, as calm as you would part from a ghost
you have no belief in.

I would say you were built
from fourteen parts — mouth and legs, hooves,
three piebald shapes of land,
chest and heart.

Marsh Angels

Horses, pale as bone   pale as snow,
    wick and wild, who would think such bodies
  could live on waves?   Live where the water writes
such a faint line between its cool length and bleached pages
                of sky
     where water makes the horses seem
to come alive twice —   once above, cannon deep and once
      again beneath — a rippled self — blurred
   disturbed by the droplets falling from its own soft mouth —
           a self
it seems to kiss   whenever it stoops its milky cobble of a head
       to drink.
Horse has found its own way to never be   alone.
     The water holds so many mirrored friends
      so gently asking nothing more
   than to be beloved to another.
    There is no cost but standing here   or running here —
no price for peace
      but moon, reflected moon, reflected clouds, stars,
      ribbons of hardy delta grass.
The water dries upon them like second skin.   Salt skin, silver skin.
   They are not afraid to live as ghosts —   babies born
          in fading pelts
        standing
     at their dam's side like a beautiful stain.
The Camargue's Cradle holds them safe   holds their tails like spray
     against the wind —
  holds their speed   their love.
   their resting weight.   The sand keeps
   the echoes of their feet.

As the horse made one slow orbit of its land

I place each swaying daisy-cutter step, idle through the grass.
There is a universe of truth between palm and maw. I can smell
gentleness. You bale me meadows. I bruise them between
my teeth. My skin is miracles. It ripples against a satellite of flies.
Intent and ruminant, I turn simple blades to great flesh,
wear my mane clotted to my neck, where rain has nurtured
little fruits of dew. The fence wire hooks at skeins. Sometimes,
I ship you on my spine, brace against your weight, knock stars
from the steel that you nail to my feet. Muscles work me,
suck-and-popping from poached ground – the feather
limp upon each heel is stained and suffered brown.
You see yourself on the planet of my eyes, each iris hooped
with prey-fear white. Beware, for I am bolt and heels,
the quick and yellow rip of tilted teeth.

Ceridwen

Into my crochan I have tipped
    the whole of the words I know   The best words
wybren ehediad merch grym mynydd môr
Inside this scalding croth all poems are born   all hiraeth   all hud
  all mytholeg   Inside is the taste of wisdom
I give you rhyme   I give you line and verse   I give you
the body of a   hebog dyfrgi milgi sgwarnog
Try the ideas of them   in your mind   upon your skin
Try the ideas of pelt or feather   sing through a throat of grass
of blood   of river   of air   I will boil this poetry into your bones
gobaith in every drop that you drink   awen inside even
the smallest grain   Fill your page with an ocean   shrink your poems
around the spiral of a shell   I will find you wherever you hide
  I will make my home in your head

Notes

Crochan	cauldron	Wybren	sky, heavens
Ehediad	bird	Merch	woman, daughter
Mynydd	mountain	Môr	sea
Croth	womb	Hiraeth	longing
Hud	magic	Mytholeg	mythology
Hebog	falcon	Dyfrgi	otter
Milgi	greyhound	Sgwarnog	hare
Gobaith	hope	Awen	inspiration

Thwarted Belongingness (A Pandemic Funeral)

After Thwarted belongingness and perceived burdensomeness… Van Orden et al.

a car rolls past   hushed and sleek & all stiff colloquies hush
at the sight of its elongated dark   drizzle clings to its roof
like a coat of pearls that only moments ago belonged to the sky
a spray of orchids clings   almost the length of the casket's lid
our tall friend is somehow folded up inside   none of them

belong anymore to blood or soil   the blooms sham life
when they are brought into the bitter day   how small death
has made him   what happened to the size of his laugh
we all stand in our own   wheels of space   & all I want
is to ruin the immaculate glass with my damp palm

& blur my view of the box   that once belonged to living oak
all I want is to tell him *time to get up*   & see him duck the lintel
of our door   again   I see his weeded wife & I am amazed at how
she stands   her black chiffon   flies like a tail no longer
attached to the bird   everyone remembers how he loved to sail

an umbrella domes the name of some brewery in The Lakes   so many
signs of water   puddles the shape of Buttermere   Red Tarn
leaves   falling   like soft prophets   mark the silver
with mild green boats   each no longer part of the whole crown
a voice turned metal by tannoy says   *join in the chorus*

the words are in the memorial book   & he is smiling on the cover
I lay my finger over his jaw   without his grin his face is only
a plain shell *We'll meet again*   there are cracks in the way
we all sound   & the woe on a mourner's cheek is no longer
a part of their eye   a pigeon   grey and lone settles

the chapel's ridge   its wings no longer part of flight   I look past
where a stone crop grows   above where   human seeds are sown
as I sang   my mouth filled with rain &   the wind took
each word from the ledge of my lip &   the sigh
that I made   was no longer part of my breath

I'm afraid of the ghost of Egas Moniz

I hate my mouth. How many times have I been
in   convenient? Every moment is a wall. What on Earth did I say
tod ay? My tongue is a heifer's foot. It navigates the ground
like   catastrophe. There's always shit on the tip. Catch me
befor   e I am hung on the scaffold of dusk, mumbling curses,
learnin   g how they taste, thick on the lip, vulgar and salty as cum,
how th   ey creep, quiet and corrupt to the grike of my ear.
I hate my   words. Every second thing is a muttered *cunt*
or *fuck*, a   nd nobody hears (I hope) my strange-dulcet obloquies.
He would h   ave cut me from my mouth, made it somehow sweet.
I forgot how   to go anywhere. Forgot how to dress. He would have
spiked my bra   in, needled me neat. This person I know said
they could unde   rstand, *the gays. Lesbians even* (though
they said it throu   gh the skin of their teeth, all shamed at the saying.
But the ones who   want both are the worst of all. Something badly
wrong with them, s   hould be shot. This person I know would have
sent me to him. *Plea   se, Mr Moniz, can you poke the bisexual out?*
And I do wonder. My   own ideates of lust have nothing to do with
tool or cleft. If I want y   ou, it's because I think you are wonderful,
because you made me fe   el like stars, because we'd go together like
beetroot and pixies, becau   se I want to believe in your glorious bones.
If he could have got his ha   nds on me, he would have spired
my socket, left a dream of st   eeples in the corner of my eye.
I would have been sent to him   for the variance, the appetite, the ugly
musings of my skull. He woul   d have cured me with his bright,
amazing spear, done me for a h   usband – meek and muzzled frumpy,
cut me down to a dull sparrow, ha   d me subtle as a wing. He might
have found me already filled with n   ails. Mr Moniz was busy
making us well. Do you kn ow he wo   n the Nobel Prize for breaking
heads? Some quack with a hammer wo   uld have cleaned you from
my cortex. I would not learn your skin's   delicious song. He would have
left no room for angels. Would have punc   tured me mild as bread.

I see you | hold the secrets of myself

To my ancestor-grandmother Brigid

I see you | walk the Wicklow Mountains | wind at the hem
of your shawl | its tassels blown alive | its wool hazed
with wetting rain | your feet bare | heels granite hard
on those soft shades of green | your hair stripped

from rusty pins | wild slicks clinging | your freckled brow
your chest strong | arms brawn | your smell of earth and sweat
your gaze slanted | up to where | a peregrine claims the air
I believe that you loved birds | living so near

to the Great Sugar Loaf | reminds you of hunger | of bread
I see you | measure the pebble shore | each sinking step
an answer to your weight | salt on your tongue | and the sand
and the wide sky | I see you take the path to mass | call to your kin

collar scoured lye bright | careful in your good boots
your early morning breath | like the shape of an angel
did you hear much Hell | on your day of rest
I see you press your palm | to the vacant ambry

of Old Conna's ruined church | like the relic of a saint
perhaps you come here to think | of your sister's ghost | or as one
of a house of twelve for peace | I see you | perched on a stool
outside to catch the best light | sprigging bloom to linen

apron a map of the day's stains | dirt between your toes | I see you
watch the grate and clop of a passing cart | greet the driver with
a pale smile | the moon looks above your home | reads you with
an ethnographic eye | I see the meagre comfort of the hearth

fire | smoke | scent | the dream of water away in the corries
of Lough Bray | their blue circles kept like gems | the Dargle
speaks you | a river's silver hymn | the taste of plain potatoes
in your mouth | and in your mind the man you loved

who took your name | gifted to you at a Kingstown font
as his bride-price | and you made the child | who made the child
who crossed the sea to Liverpool | who made the child
who made the mother | who in the end | made me

Jeanne, Visions, Trousers, Flames

The Castle of Rouen, eve of execution, 29th May, 1431

Because I love the dusk, I have carved myself this sacred time to watch,
squirrelled these moments from the waste of my worried days. I lay
the warmth of my palm to my aching neck as the sky sheds the day,
as nearby trees moult the light like shades of velvet from their boughs.
Birds strip their flight from the air, submit to the roost and leave night
to the moths. Tonight would be a good time for visions. All the years
I've had them, it's now I need them most. Send me a dream of pale horses,
wild and spattered with broken marsh. Show me my old Domrémy home,
where the corn spired to the sun's gold, where rain used to cool
my parent's tilted house. No more plagues of fighting. Please,
no more saints. They saw me ride astride, saw me wearing trousers.
I live these last few hours, as darkness drowns my tower. Send an illusion
of courage that I might pray real. I want to know how much it will hurt
when they kindle my feet, when they dress me in heretic's flames.

In November   2021

I found my past between the lines   on census forms   in passenger lists
funny how we always leave   parts of ourselves behind   are we ever
really dead?   perhaps someone   a million years from now will sift
through documents for me   my birthright is words   let me leave you
an inheritance   of magpie tales   like how in November   2021
at the side of the A685   (Kirkby Stephen)   I saw a bare winter tree
instead of leaves   it was hung with pairs of shoes   apparently
they are there for hope   though what shoes have to do with hope
is anyone's guess   maybe they mean   *I hope you can   escape*
I hope you might stay   or it just seemed like the natural thing to do
at the time   what does this have to do with my finding of kin?   nothing
more than stumbling upon something interesting because I happened to   look
maybe nothing more than   people come   people go
and all they leave behind are   curious traces

metapoem / iteration (Dickinson, 568)

We learned the Whole of Love— / The Alphabet—the Words—
Diviner than the Childhood's— / And each to each, a Child—

Love, spent between paper — Child becomes   elemental
a is $^1/_5$ of apple, aphid, abyss — Child keeps atoms in their head
Alpha   *so which*, Child asks, *is the best Book?*   **Omega**
if **A**   is for a pristine block   and **Ω**
for messy margin notes,   a ruined tombola of highlighting pen,

then this lesson,   Child says,   *is an apocalypse*
bcdefghijklmn o   pqrstuvwxy z   each page a feather from
an Angel's wing — Divine — falling upon incomprehension,
unknowledge,   made   knowledge,   made   beautiful,
made fear   Courage (reified) is a shadow on the side of a horse

                    in the shape of a fist
if reif (Scottish, obsolete, noun) is [the spoils of] learning, then Child
has stolen from these books   if reif (German, adj.) is ripe, at last
then, Child's mind is ready   if re is somehow Latin *thing,*

then Glorious!

now they may speak such *thingifications*   and learning comes,
Divine!   Child is searching bone dry ground,   pulling portents
from gore   and *careful now!*   Child is
    hy - poth - e - sis - ing (gerund)   their way to Truth —
Truth, says Child, *is the presence of air,*   is the maker of flame,

    is written into each leaf's fold   *Truth,*
says Child, *is possibly fallacious,*   not only to be found
    in God's garden — the snake's head,   the oyster's eye

    seek the elucidation of scented library shelves
    papyrus   plume   skin   and liquor scars

Bear   ii   sometimes bear, sometimes poems, sometimes love

in the dark she has churned like fat milk, rolled to ease   the pressure
of self   rolled again, rolled eleven times an hour, rolled twelve
restless she, comfort stays indifferent here   truant season, roasted she
in podgy fug   summer long, she ate a wealth, each berry-calorific page,
each honey book, clawed each silver image out from shallow brook,
synecdoche of sweet flesh   (stash of notebooks future-full of cobbled
junk)   tried to turn a gobble-weight of poems into euphonies of sleep
deliberate prisoner she   plugged the cavern's door with a year
of unwanted things   spoiled citations, one request to she for exegesis
(kneel on stones and holy *fuck*), erasers that left a filthy smear, rejections,
typos, bubbles of verse that taunt the night and burst before she gropes
the room for necessary ink   she lets this clutter close her in
reading she, buttering theory round her barrel mind   hopes some bits
will stick to the sides   some poems are warm at least   some great
remembered lines and some are made as monuments, a bulk of sand,
unconquerable fells   waiting, much less patient she   and sudden,
something about the change of light, subtle as flame so many miles
away   sudden finds that some day   is *this* day   time
to build the stones of body back to upright shapes, to ripple out
her heavy pelt, shake all wreckage from its greedy sea, time to find water
goodbye   she says, *goodbye*   to cave that sweats a season's mess
of dreams   *goodbye* to bed of leaves that learned to dent beneath
her frame   *thank you* for the space it gave for she to think   *thank you*
for a winter's safe   casserole of thrice-known breath, of gross wind,
of all-too-familiar scents   *thank you* for the rest it took to swallow
up her musty tongue   spit she out as empty shell and start
a whole new hunger in her head, gawking over fresh and vivid meat
she looks although the sky seems much too full   and maybe,
somewhere past that mountain   love

I hadn't heard poetry read out loud before, or talked about as if it was a Real & Important Thing until a brilliant teacher made it so

IMO Miss Moss, Barnsley 6ᵗʰ Form College, 1987

I remember her so clearly — her smiling moon-shaped face,
stringy fawn hair, huge-framed glasses
(the kind that sit oddly upside-down upon the nose),
damp earnest eyes, psalmic voice,
long skirts, stout shoes.
When I say that she reminded me of dust
I mean a beautiful kind of dust —
the kind that settles gently around you,
like love.

We read poems by Smith, Heaney and Betjeman
(I can still recite almost the whole
of *A Subaltern's Love Song* by heart) —
his words *mushroomy, pine-woody* are a part
of my most beloved echolalia mechanisms.
It's especially good to repeat while walking
(I believe the poem laid foundations concerning the mouthfeel and rhythm
of poetry inside future me).

Mushroomy, pine-woody mushroomy, pine-woody
mushroomy, pine-woody. I did not know then
that I would grow up to be a poet.
She opened each word like a flower —
I sort of understood yet didn't quite understand
what she meant, back then.
True appreciation of what she did for me came after.
What a shame we can't travel back in time
and thank people like this —

show them we did amount to something in the end.
What do you think it means, the teacher asked,
to be that far out and drowning?
It means somebody like me is sitting in a lesson like this
somewhere right now and this new sea has swallowed
them up and swilled a shock of salt around their head,
I thought but dared not say. They can taste
the water's breath, the lightness of the chrism oil
upon its blessed skin.

Pantoum to Maud's Absolutely Brilliant Door

After *Maud and Everett Lewis*, photograph by Kathleen Hooper, 1960s

there on her door   the life of the sky   as if the wood had wings
she could shut out   the cold   close herself in and   still
be flying one scuffed chair hardly bruised by small weight   her things
upon a table   waiting for glad hands to gather each brush and fill

frugal pulpboard with   rich life she could close herself in and still
make a life of miracles paint windows   into an Eden of her own
upon a table   waiting for curled hands to lift each brush and fill
her home with bloom   daylight turned to flowers   four walls grown

into a garden   behind the shingles   she drew an Eden of her own
bread box, cupboard, mirror, stove   radiant beyond   the use
expected of them   Maud leans against the frame   but four walls grow
strong around her   loneliness   poverty and pain   transduce

into pages bright with truth   her tools lie, almost   beyond use
bristles bent from making   oxen, child, water, snow a bluebird
seems to bump into Everett's head   flies against poverty   transduces
altered mobility into   the freedom of air   she preferred

her colours unblurred, undimmed   on the timber's snow   a bluebird
a butterfly, bumblebee   a yellowbird, blackbird   a redbird bring
her the freedom of air   could not leave her behind   she preferred
them on her door   the whole life of the sky   as if the wood had wings

Imagined Letters Between Emily Dickinson / Joseph Cornell / Myself About 405 /

Toward The Blue Peninsula

Dear Emily   I
am empty of birds   I saw This Room
& I thought of My own   — *Blue Seclusion* —
I am either asking You to come in
or I have already let You out   & in the End
it has only ever been about the Waiting
An Interior Of Nothing   An Interior of
Everything   like a cell   like a retreat
like a rejection   a hole in an Angel's Wing
cadaver cold   studied & stripped of beating
Heart & bloated Lung   Whose life is only painted plain —
Whose life is love made Algebraic —

    Dear Joseph   I
    knew, before I even saw Your Box
    that it would have a Window   You must
    have thought (like I thought)   when We
    read *That* Poem   that there *had* to be
    a Secret Code   something to do with Rooms
    & Seclusion   & the Vital Importance
    of A View   We learned those Words
    — *My Blue Peninsula* —   & turned
    Our heads   like She must have turned
    Her head ·   toward the wall
    & its Sky-borrowed Sight —

Dear Emily   I
have built this   — *Blue Redemption* —
This is how I reach   You
Woman on the wrong side of Sky
I offer You this Gouge of Bone
this home-made Utopia   Notice
that I left enough Room for God
I give You such Infinitudes of Small
the Freedom of Confine   the Worship
of Seclusion   & Peace (if We can find it)
If We did   would We want it —
What use is Company for People like Us —

　　　Dear Joseph   I
　　　can't help but imagine Your bleached
　　　& perfect hollow spoiled by tears   or skin
　　　or pubic hair   or blood   or screams
　　　I think about all those Birds you kept
　　　the painted Flight on wooden Wings
　　　the stifling of Song   & You   as Master
　　　of their Fate   as   — *Blue Blasphemy* —
　　　There is something so Beautiful
　　　about being so artfully Trapped   everything Large
　　　can be a Prisoner   every view
　　　can be moored   — Whose life is only sky —

Dear Emily   · I
imagine You writing to Him   and Me
in the middle   writing to Both & all
with heads full of Hermitage
& We talk about Ravens   Patterns   Bubbles
or   — *Blue Banishment* —
How Wonderful   Incredible   Beautiful
that   We somehow fit this assemblage
of Neat Things—   I see Your pen
screwing Your Freedom into aphoristic lines
while *Salaratus* & Your hands
work Your Bread with living Air —

      Dear Joseph   I
      learn this new threshold that I
      without the Body's weight may now cross
      You made a Room of Snow   invented
      the difficult shape of wires   Worship milked
      upon the walls   & Outside   — *Blue Amnesia* —
      I folded all of Myself into each Page
      Poet's Jasmine growing Wild   beyond
      Westfield Seek-No-Furthers grown fat
      & content   lading the branches around
      the Bobolink's Song —
      each fascicle straining for Sky

Ocular Map   To Mary's Paper Garden

O!

    Mary Ellen Solt   now
I read you   corm to crown   I have seen
an illumination   you & your flowers
    O!   Mary Ellen Solt   how could I
I realise that I am   not alone   imagine
a cultivar   not seeing you
  seeing   Mary Ellen Solt   this fear of
your flowers   label me   blaspheming
 is like   your apostle   the page
seeing God

      I saw   I need to own
  I crave   your poems   the things
  you grow like incredible weeds   you wrote
I think   each poem is   a universe
  I would like a constellation   right there
  to break   in front of my eyes
upon your grave like a wave   or if you were
    O!   Mary Ellen Solt   burned
petals to ashes   breath to brain   let your flowers
  brain to heart   heart to hand   Come to me
  hand to pen pen to page   upon the air
    O! I saw   page to poem
  your fragrant miracles   each blank sheet blooms

  let me make   M   a   petals
   this offering   r y E l   on concrete
at the altar   l   e   n   suffering
  of your words S   o l   surviving
offer this   t   speaking the truth
  Ocular Map with you   a treasure   of the rose
   kept inside like a relic   I see
  each letter a seed   nascent   boundaries grown wild
  on pale soil   wheels of marigold

                    a web of forsythia   Mary Ellen Solt
            a verse shaped from more than words   has written
        shaped from root and filament   the wind
            O for Ovule   into each stem
            becoming as light   shaping itself scion
            as leaves   I see you speak
                           as only a living thing would
            in the space between   your language
            is a garden   is pure as the air
            a sweet gathering
        orthography bloomed   upon
                    a fertile frame

Elizabeth's Fish

see me flail upon the riverbank   I cannot breathe   I said
my body's long brawn   unwatered   denuded   will wear itself wretched
on this mud   won't somebody come   and tip me back   ?
tell me a story   suggests the sky   while you work out whether to die
or live   so here's a curious thing   I said   I met Elizabeth Bishop's fish
saw its rack of mouth   punctured many times with shank and barb
its mouth the sound of needles and tin   it spoke its fate through flits
of ragged fin   it made the occasional cumbersome plunge   aimed
the alloy roll of each sardonic eye toward my head   what is there left
said the fish   for me   but being pulled every now and then
into strange realms   ?   do you really wish to follow me there   ?
I am nothing more   said the fish   than a ghost   awake when the book
is opened   erased when the book is closed   my tatty skin can still
bear a rainbow   read me   leaping from each line   get up
go home and start to write   you can still be luminous   said the fish
the sun will strike your sides   your language will be light
there are some who will always answer you   said the fish   with rod
with line   they will try to catch you no matter what you do
answer them with the bones that you shape   with your pen
but for now   said the fish   lie still   it's not all about fighting
lie still   said the fish   and learn the ways of air
lie still my tremendous friend   and take it in

On Writing an Acceptance to the Self

write a gallon of it from your heart . leave it a week . go back and flay
it lean with your head . leave it a week . be awful strict . toil it raggy .
smooth it with an adoring hand . let it settle . like cream on milk . snow
on filth . salt on chips . let it m e t a m o r p h o s e .
polish it proud . you should be proud . of yourself . for having the courage
to pick up a pen . for carving out this precious time for yourself .
for sticking your head above the parapet . discover the curious notion
of competition . of submission . of duelling with words . get hurt .
get utterly bruised . get happy sometimes . get hurt . and hurt again .
get happy . hurt again . happy again . write yourself an email .
be your own validation . accept yourself . write and you already won .
use it as an antidote to those messages that begin with . *I regret to inform you* .
close but no cigar . *we enjoyed reading your work but* . send it to yourself
whenever you stop believing you are a writer . send it to yourself
when you stop believing in your own tongue . when you feel yourself
hemmed by notions that everyone else might be better . more successful .
more valued . than you . when it seems much too dark outside and in .
sit down . *sit right down and write . myself a letter* . if it's good enough
for Joe Young . it's good enough for you . or better still . send it
to a friend . one you know is doubting themselves just the same .
and when you . or they . see this email . their . or your . pulse . will
beat . and beat . and beat . and for a moment you . or they . can ride
that terrible . dangerous . wonderful tidal wave of hope . when you .
or they . see those first delicious lines . *congratulations you have won* .
your poem has been . accepted for this issue . we are delighted . your poem
will go . on a journey to the moon and back . will be given a necklace
of flowers . a gaudy medal . a crown . an extra slice of gooey cake .
your poem will be . already is . a Great and Important Thing . don't forget
to sign off with . take care . best wishes . with all due respect . sincerely .
I love you . I fucking love you . top of the morning . keep shining .
faithfully . and all that jazz . use a different font for your signature .
you crazy thing . because you wrote it . because there is more to life
than 12 pt Times New Roman . because you took it from your skin .
and laid it on a page . because nobody else could have done . or will do
what you have done . because it is your DNA . because poems are gifts .
and have made . or will make . a difference to your life .
or even just to someone else's day .

How to Write a Competition Poem

The best poems will always be about birds — the quills spearing
their hide; how it feels to fledge with nails. Murmurations are more
than flight looping mass to the clouds — they are a thought's unsolvable
knot; the mind's wing; an antidote to dusk. The best poems will always be
about sky — how it hangs its weight above our heads; how it greys

or blues or storms in tune to our latest discontent; how our pain
becomes a sherd in the sediment of night; how it begins to rain
and all we can think of is tears. The best poems will always be
about loss, for a poem is a room in which trauma is kept — a room
where desolation shall be remade as mirror, window, empty

old beloved chair, untended dust, or slanted curtain light.
The best poems will always be about journeys we take — the distances
from war to peace; fathoms beneath a small boat's hull; the courage we need
to travel through life and let our stories out; a pilgrimage of hours —
history passed from mouth to memory; tablet to papyrus;

a treasured book of recipes; alt text to braille. The best poems
will always be in a borrowed creature's voice — from tardigrade to whale
and all the bodies tame or wild between — without a hare's mystery,
how would we alloy self and pelt? *I lost my mother*, the ungulate said,
and my sorrows have made me forget the meaning of milk.

Without the deer's frailty, how would we speak our bones?
Our words are horses — we are solved when we morph ourselves
into myth. The best poems will always be about grief. Poems are friends
that stop us falling from the chasm's edge; are a mapping of unknowns —
tinctures, thimblerigs. We write our way out of each raw stage —

the eighth stage is the story of how I wept in the Post Office queue;
the tenth is not knowing who I'm meant to feed. Now that you are gone,
there seems no need to eat. The best poems will always be green.
Every time we sing the sway of grass, verse the shifting dunes, the hope
of trees, or scribe our shame to mountains the planet smiles.

The best poems will always be about the sea, for we have dressed our skin
in transmutations of salt. The best poems are beautiful — are filled
with rage; moons and constellations, stone and silt, moss, and mushroom,
psalms and one palm, gloved from the cold and held against my own.
I remember your eyes; everything you said about truth, trust, and time.

The best poems are blades. They will always be about love.

Strophe/Antistrophe/Epode/
to being all the parts of me inside a poem

Hush my mouth ! Excuse me if I
talk in shapes of flower , if my
tongue tastes of rainbows . I might
even dabble the list of Naughty Poet
words — fish out a dose of
weft-heft-plash-Jesus ?! soul
(*rainbow* also *hark* and heck knows
how many more) . *Epiphany* and
Hell no ! I won't live without that
Bug the hell out of folk . Use
'em . Liberate 'em . Write
wot the F U like . The poems I
write are the footprints I leave
behind . I love my paper and pen
— what's a mistake or two
between friends ? I love the
juicy bone of an adjective , how I
love to wrap my florid lips around
vivid ideas of abstract noun .
Pulchritudinous soundings of verb!

But find ye plain / soft and safe / be gentle
still / speak only in the necessary things /
bring gentle mouth / be subtle still / as bird is lost
to mild sky / turn from this chaotic self / shrine
each word / the page a mim altar / be
humble still / for Words are God / and you

only a cell for them to echo in / fear
your bite / swallow the sword of your
tongue / inside you is a shameless
twin / soothe her frenzied hair / be prayer
and pilgrim / quiet / be quiet / be not in
thrall to a metaphor's wink / hull
your verse to bare pip / be still

The page lent its wide, unwritten mouth. *In this space, find absolution,*
it said. And I was kind/unkind to myself. My dissolution
came and it wore a coat of words. *We will destroy you. Remain*
calm, my chick. Through us you can build yourself again.

Interoception

I am lying straight and keeping   very still   relishing the weight
of the blankets above pressing on my flesh.   *Can you not feel your bladder*
flinch?   Hurry!   before you void an ocean, before you piss your bed

It's time for my daily paradigms   Every morning, early-riser I   haunt
these kind, unpopulated hours for as long as I can   prise the shell
of my bruxism splint from my night-milled teeth — their plastic echo is chewed
almost through.   I cannot avoid last night's smeared plates — somebody else's
snow of crumb's.   Every single morning, I think   *this is not the place*
where I live   this olfactory input nightmare stink   *Oh but it's so lovely*
and quiet   says my sensation-avoiding self   *when nobody else is up*

No banging, no hammermouthfartshoutargument noise   *How are you*
feeling today?   I don't know. I don't   *Where*, I said *is my homeostasis?*
I grip my hand to the table   This is my vestibular pain   I feel

the floor's imperceptible downward tilt   like the princess felt the pea   Oh
myheadmyheadmy head   *come to the cool of the tabletop, forehead to flat*
Tell yourself   that you will not be thrown from the surface of the world

I think therefore   therefore, therefore I am   alone. Come   go away
shut up. Please stay   Descartes proved his existence because   he doubted
his existence   The moments I doubt myself are the moments that make me
alive   Don't touch me. I am untouchable   This couple on the bus
all touchy-feely are making me want to scratch beneath   my own skin

I will show you I love you in ways that do not fall   so easily from the tongue
I am a thousand miles from where we are   I am   alexithymia's wall
Oh beautiful loneliness   There is no room on the seat next to me
I am sorry, sorry   My handbag is Cerberus. My heart batters against its cave

I am afraid that my mouth will form the first thought that pops into my head
If only I could un-say the already said   Must I always be a mirror?

If I was a river I would be guided by my banks   If I was contours on a map
I would write the shape of the land   find every possible path.   A bird would
know the exact requirements of sky, how to breathe blue   how to sing
the right notes   how to synchronise with the murmuration's swoop.

                                                Perhaps.

I am Road, I am Mother, I am a Better Person Now, I am Failed

So I have this ache to run.

      I just got sick, sick of the sight of myself, sick
of the unpleasant feelings of flesh. I have dreamed this cumbrance away,
spent too much of this elongated time
on my back (imagining sky) wishing my grody molecules would buzz
away like a bluebottle cloud. When was the last time
I properly slept? I get rid of portions of the dark — scald my corneas
on some book.   Fail to feel the words go in. Forget
what I have read. Masturbate. Not because I'm thinking *sex*.
I have to find something buried in myself
      like trying to get to the beat in a dead bird's breast.
              The rest of the time
I turn like a bundle of sticks, go numb, turn the cogs
on morsels from the previous day, or leave them void.
My eyes swell like storm drains. When I hear the dawn, I cry
for the squandering of another night. I want to clamber out of this skin.
It weighs me like wet wool.
           I have crept, a fat automaton,
fridge to window, hall to bathroom, cupboard to bed. Have pacified
my family with mountains of bread. Have eaten my way
into pain. I want my bones. I want myself to carve her bright way back.
So I say to my son *let's run*. I don't say *let's run away from ourselves*.
I think I broke for good. All I can think of is how many shitty things I said.
I didn't know is no excuse and now I do, I see that my tongue
has been a cudgel, an evil fish.
              I kneel beneath an accusation of sky,
say *help me, help me please* for I have had enough
of this kind of life. *Smile, smile, smile, smile, smile.*
      So me and my son, we run. I found a road
where hardly anyone goes — no time these days for God —
Those that need wine and wafer,   suffer your sin in silence.
Go without.
Past the Shrine of the two Virgins — I have worshipped

their crumbling prayer, their sad relics, their concrete knees.
At least somebody got round to painting them
fresh again, hung baskets of flowers on each side. I stagger past
and wish for selfish things — *MaryMothers, make me thin,*
MaryMothers,   put out the pains in my head.
In front, my tall son.
Me behind, running upon the long cast of his shadow, like he's
getting away and forever I'm failing to catch him up.

Eliza save yourself from Higgins run

After the musical adaptation [of *Pygmalion*] *My Fair Lady*

your worth will be measured in speech   the voice's delicate
weight, its perfection of vowels   you must bend your lips
to the right shape, mock   yourself proper, strip

your true sound   you feel him   flinch at your eruptions
you must not call up hurricanes, must part from   your swank
feathered hat, gimcrack silks   must be pulled up by the roots

be rinsed of the sin of streets   be shriven of vulgarities
once you were poor and proud   unafraid, loud with life
he will twist you ideal   master your tongue   drive

your accent out   your idiom   you birthright of words worried
smooth, like the flawless song   of a morning bird, you
will be schooled into a fairytale   you are, to him, everything

you deserve to be   *creature, guttersnipe, low   no right to live*
he will name your class   you will know your shame, such
emphasis on cleanliness   drab Eliza, dull Eliza, filth

and curse Eliza   you shall be polished to a new pin   weaned
from these dialogues of dirt, you   must put your jaw to soft sermons
tame your inheritance, balance   your head like a dull moon

swallow your noise   he will carve your mouth   to a shy font
bend you nice   docile and good, your flailing gone   your tongue
hushed   you will be impeccable   he will allow you to be new

a most precious thing, sparkled round   your wrists and head, silent
as stone, to be offered to the room   a pretty gift, milk and spindle
throat filled up with gems, your future   an experiment by men

you wanted a room to feel safe   to make a business of your own
Eliza, spit that meal of glass   dance all night if you want to
Eliza, you and   *your bloomin' arse*   are perfect as you are

Hare cannot stop looking at a photograph of E.R. Fightmaster in a meadow

Doe is desire   under / belly me / a form   my paws have
pulled it to bare earth   soil / dark colour   to smells   of raw
of dirty / clean   of sweet   Doe is   peccant
idle / hot and nipple / down on   marl   and quivers

over tonic / cool   look to the way   they lie / like someone
threw them   into flowers and   they landed in
the shape of someone who   doesn't give
the smallest amount of fucks   and they look

like they always meant   to make a bed of   bloom
Like they're telling you   *absolutely room here*
for   two   Doe is   agog   sees their long / dangle
holding of   one thin sweet stalk   See how they keep it

to the corner of their mouth   they growl   they grrrrr
Doe says   come lip to my lip / imagines   the taste of
foxy sneer   imagines the taste   of wild
Doe is   the pity of breeze   through hoar / soft pelt

like the feel   of travelling breath   Doe is wife / is mother
is fear / is traitor   to the sight   of one crooked thigh
the idea of leaf and   skin   Doe is closing her eyes
for their T-shirt looks   just like a cathedral of   pain

Ocular Map   Three Interpretations

After *Elixir*, by Pipilotti Rist, 2009

Two
　drowned women
not drowned　　　There
half drowned　　　are trees　Yet now
drowning in the　　hanging　　I think I see
shape of a 69　　from the sky　　two women
　in the scent　at first I thought　foetal above
of one other　I saw beautiful water　the turning
in the unmistakable　now I see　　of the world
　river taste　their love upon　they could be
and their hair　a forest floor　great angels
ran out behind them　and now their hair　Cherubim above
like quick red fish　is red as leaves　the doors of Eden
like the flaming pelt　like the blooming　the patron saints
of two creatures　of two roses　of Queer Love, hung
like banners proclaiming　like living scarlet　like pride, like
　love　wings　atmosphere
and their bodies　and their skin　and each spine
curled like babies born　is young as if life　will hold them
and suddenly grown　has just begun　you must be
　like kittens who play　the shape of fear　beneath them
like untethered weed　is trapped inside　to know the feel
a solution of woman　the square of light　of them floating
perhaps they only seem　shadows like　ghosts and flesh
to be floating　creeping things　perhaps they are sisters
like spiders　　or friends
waiting like　strangers who cling
at the end of the world
and all we can do
is lie beneath them
and look

Afterwinter

Blackthorn blossom — sweet, humble, clustered, wedding-coloured —
in profusion. On a morning like this it is soft and cold, each bloom the size

of a thumbnail. Each petal made from fabric so thin it can hardly be felt —
almost like the smallest disturbance of air, the breath of a sleeping child.

Filaments lift from each corolla's core, fine as thread — every one of them
topped with a pinhead ball of gold. The scent is honey marvellous —

will make you dream of bees. Be mindful of the spikes, for blackthorn
is as brutal as it is beautiful — like a person you wish still loved you

being held against the pity of your unwanted love. Before the leaves,
it grows its flowers — seems eager to have them blanketing its plain bark

and bough. Perhaps, in winter's wake, an awareness of nudity comes
and inflorescence is thrown over the top of its bones, like something

old-fashioned, almost forgotten — bloomers over legs. A shelf
edged with lace. Against my hand it seems exactly like the snow.

if I was the tiny seahorse   clung

if I gave myself to the heave
    of the sea   went under its weight
if my mouth held all the odours of wrack
    eddied with ruddy dulse   the savour

of kelp's drowned forests   the sapor of foam
    if I opened my lips to all the tastes
of blue   became the everything of water
    bound the planet in my rolling skin

if I spread myself like a living sheet of glass
    filled my womb with fin and wreck
my storm of a body   foraging outlines of land
    if I hid my own flesh

inside a whelk's long muscle   became
    its supple quest   layered my nakedness
with shields of shell   cockled myself in
    slumped my body along its nacre walls

if I were oceans   the swallowed portent
    of whalesong   the miracle of krill
if I swarmed beneath the moon   swelled inside
    a luminescent wash   wore a radiant meniscus

if I was a deep and permanent cold   a lorn bulk
    of sheer bergs   if I slept beneath a coat of torn floes
wore ribbons of aurora in my rippled hair
    buoyed the pale mass   of great bears

if I made my head into an urchin's hollow globe
    and let the hoard of everything   I have lost
remain as ghosts   if I was all the tiny horses   clung
    like herds of hope to threads of weed

if I was an anemone's shy head   if I made a curious home
      of benthic depth   aimed for the lure
of distant light   if I was a gull's drifting breast
      an eternity of salt

I told the Horse a long, long story of the dark

I have written my days around the teapot   Smell the tannins on my tongue
I'm losing all that I ever liked about myself   I am coming, as I always do
to your big hot neck   Your speckled hide   If I was to tell you
This gate — I could kick it down   Do you think I cannot clear
this cursory fence   You have come to ask me why I stay — I guess
the exchange of confine for comfort   never having to wonder where the next
How gentle you are, massive friend   Though you have the strength
to crush my bones I know that you won't   You test my skin for scent
drink your fill of my breath
Strange that I make some people afraid — I am all the raw and wild
everything you have forgotten about yourself   The years you have brought
your broken self to my side and said
I believe you love me — you answer when I call   it seems as if you do
My shadow acts upon your flank   You have captured my shape on your hide
It weighs nothing   The sky is a burden on our backs
How tenderly you take the thistle from my tail, the old stems of curly dock
I remember when you took me to the body of my dead friend   You imagined
you were helping me to understand my grief   Winter is when everything seems
Winter is when we layer with fat and coat   *Hello, horse*   I made a mother
of the dark   a lover of the dark—   I made a long, long story of the dark
There is a kind of music around my house   Who else but you could I tell that to
I dream of green. Though I am hay full   I am sick of tasting the ghosts
of summer   The land is echoes   I dream in wolves   Can winter sing
from my long, long throat?
I made a question of the dark — it bared its chest for my pen and I wrote
whatever would serve for an answer   *How clever you are*   said the dark
as it rolled its body on top of my world and crushed it dim
Do you see how I have used my teeth to cut out the stars   I am the sound
of castles running on the frozen rut and bog   My voice will astonish
will rankle through this forsaken day   The sun is low to nothing
I made a catastrophe of the night   pulled it around me like a dull crépe dress
You have never been more alive   said the dark   *now that you are indistinct*
You have never been more beautiful to me

When Pauline Sings Big River

"If you believe that there's a bond / Between our future / And our past /
Try to hold on to what we had" – From *Big River*, by Jimmy Nail

Have you ever watched somebody stand up and sing   no music, no strings
or symphony   stand up and sing   a little worse for wear, maybe for drink
and tune themselves back to the past   Pauline sings *Big River*   and
every line says   *gone   it's all gone   there is absolutely nothing left*

We all need a tune to hang our tears upon   I see that my friends are old
that death is feeling its way   into their flesh   they are returning
in their thoughts   to some old street   some old face   every line says

Remake the place you were happiest   oh, nostalgia   the cursed rose
that settles its tint upon the brain like bliss   like time's narcotic twin   *Big
River*   Remember   the people crying here were children   once upon a

Tyne   I saw a heron set its skinny legs   into your travelling length
build itself into a perfect embodiment of pain   I saw it   clutching
the rock like a fist clings to rage   such a long way you have come,
river   North and South to Watersmeet   then out toward the sea

Tree Breathe Leaf Shade Fruit Home Branch Wood Bird

Imagine a forest drowning in dapples. Thank the trees for shelter —
for beauty, photosynthesis, and root. For green, for the overstory layer.
Use the language of forests — deciduous, evergreen, coniferous, tropical,
boreal, temperate, montane. Imagine speaking through filaments —

feeding one another stories of danger, nutrients, health. Did you know
trees can recognise kin? Mother Trees are wisdom-broad, ages deep.
If this node is cut, the seedlings will fail. We should not break the web
beneath the ground. Intricate and nourishing, their mycorrhizal idiom

is need, not greed. I keep one hundred acres alive inside my head.
You enter through an avenue of cherries. Their petals drift my skull
like rain. A dazzle of Acers — Ukigumo, Amagi Shigure, Beni Maiko,
Katsura, Skeeter's Broom — ignite their rainbow-coloured pillow shapes.

Chestnut, hazelnut and oak drop their shining bounty. Help yourself
to my orchards of apple, pear, greengage, quince, orange and plum. Eat
yourself well. Eat till you remember sweet. The politicians here
are bees and deer, birds, and clearwings. Shaggy Brackets, bryophytes.

Their manifesto is three words brief — time, pollination, peace.
Willows hem a pond. Rowan, holly, and hawthorn hold the snow.
Flowers grow at their roots. My brain is a pinecone. I breathe needles.
Discover your favourite tree. Curl under its canopy and sleep. Read

the textures of paper birch, smooth beech, ridged ash, aspen lenticels
against your skin. Learn them through your hands. There is filtered sun.
To be immersed is to notice. To exist. To empty out your mind.
I translate this feeling as happiness. I am happiness. Happiness

comes from the throat of birds. Dawn, morning, afternoon and dusk
will arrive at any time you wish. Come back to the old ways. This
place is the only truth you will need. I hear how you flicker in your sleep.
You are safe. Untroubled and warm. Sleep

because here, truth is roots. Truth is resin, wood, and fruit — the flight
of owls. There will be a moon. The leaves will thread with constellations.
There will be an incredible night sky
                        with you beneath, supine.

All day, it rained

This evening I saw a raven drinking
from the rain gutter of the neighbour's caravan. Sometimes bad weather
does no more harm than this. I am caused to smile. Oh raven
dipping, shining raven, how
does your rillet taste?

I don't even mind this gentle wet. The pebbles in my garden
deepen in their damp skins. Such blues, browns and reds!
Such cobble-granite, quartz and sparkling white!

These pebbles are memories. I remember why I picked each one of them up.
Beloved egg shaped one, holey hag stones, moon and slub shapes;
stones plumed and cushioned with moss.
I watched a programme once about a garden in Japan,
where moss puffed and careful people knelt,
plucking out tiny stems of grass. How endlessly calm
its emerald soft emulsion would be — how nourishing
for the heart, how lenitive to touch.

A parent's hands can be the most dangerous thing you know.
I believe I could give my whole life
to the purity of moss.

To the Kilburn Horse, seen from
the Leeds to Newcastle train

Past holding tanks of human waste, past   the kind of beautiful homes
where dreams are best had, past   cows, dutifully towing their slantwise hips,
        udders like slung pink bells   between their bandy legs. Past
    rolling green,   ragged, wilful hedgerows, past   the beginning of the end
for all the leaves. Past   barracks filled with livestock — windowless,

        removed   from the knowledge of the world, drifting from birth,
    to death without light — past   the pretty beads on pumpkin fields, past
        miles of arable land, I strain until   I see the first bright flicker
of geoglyph — from this angle you look   like a huge, bemusing tooth.

The trees swallow you up and spit you out again. You are cut
    into the surface of Roulston Scar. You are the shape   where topsoil
was scraped. You are its filling   with gravel   its ghosting of lime.

Fields keep   your flesh and blood counterparts — their paddock boundaries
sketched with electric tape, their edges   worn with repetitive tread. You
        watch, with an   island   of grass for an   eye. Your muscles are rock,
            your heart a hillside.   Birds   mock the ways that we are

fastened to the land. I see   a gathering — sheep, made placid for now
are circled to a woolly clump by a dog's working speed.   The herd submits —
the dog has flattened itself to ground, ears spiked, body   a piebald Sphinx,
        face fixed to the farmer's next command.   Everything waits —
        each creature called to heel. The collie lays its gift of loyalty
            at the muddy feet of this man.

Soon the dusk will rest upon your painted hide. I will imagine   you
    as a free thing, peeling   your moonlit skin from the anchor of the moor.
I will imagine you running —   your pale self spinning over Yorkshire as if
        you were a splendid wheel, then   settling back, icon
                again before the dawn comes.

I am losing the sight of you   horse — there you are once more,
    for a last moment —   looking north. You seem, to me   to be always
            looking north.

Miracles

Blue sky clinging to glass; implausibly lime-green grass; a hoard of coins,
value extinguished by the soil, their gold against a mole's nose;
a tiny caterpillar crossing the road; a dry line of washing; bones inhumed
with bibelots; a rotted hull; tongues of garnet, each abraded quiet;
urchin fossils; rags of fabric looped into a rat's nest; undiscovered evidence
of prayer; a song on the radio you had forgotten you loved; fixing
what is broken without asking for help; a horse's back behind a hedge,
the smell of hay and flesh; a red felt plectrum; the sound of nobody outside;
the love I never had for you is a joyous thing, there is nothing about you
I wish to need; the brilliant shade of teal I painted my shelf; a halved
and empty robin's egg; I do not care a fig about your face; the liberty
of deer; I remember the importance I placed upon your hands; the jasmine
weaving over the fence; pigeons coupling with abandon in a neighbour's tree,
the hawk that will eat them; a Victorian mirror crudely daubed with flowers;
the scent of cooking rice; unseasonable warmth; a cat greasing its claim;
apple-glow; a lock of hair; the stones on the path, the way they tilt my feet.

Always Make Friends with a Cloud

After 'Never Make Friends with a Crow', by Tua Forsström

Because each one will only live for one minute to an hour,
you might be the only friend it ever has; the one to act as witness
to its life. Sad to think that some won't even get to the end of the street
before they die. How can we measure the truth of a cloud?
Most seem happy enough — drifting, misty, noctilucent, light.
Some are weights of ire but there is nothing wrong
with letting people learn your unpredictable side. This, in the end,
is the only way they break rage upon us. We forgive our friends
a bitter tongue — sometimes their blue is overcast. They cannot
always be the asepsis of ice.

Perhaps they do not need my grief. Perhaps it is enough to taste air.
Perhaps time is different for clouds —
what we know as a moment is, to them, a thousand years of sky.
Perhaps they are often glad to leave us behind. Perhaps
they make the shape of a rabbit just to see us smile.

There is a cloud, many light-years away from Earth.
It has been alive for billions of years. Great Ancestor Cloud, Deity Cloud,
will you lend your trick to these pitiful wisps? Are you their evidence
of an afterlife? Do they pity us our heavy skins;
our doubts, our ground, our weakened faith,
our own attempts to fly?
Perhaps their deaths are rain.

We are both just so much water.
Small wonder then, that we cry.

Me and the Goldsworthy, Alone

Time has reclaimed this great dream — dissolved its neat beginning
beneath three decades of grass. Time has mellowed the knolls into soft

green whales, their mossy blubber scarred by stunt-bike tyres
and scrambling feet. Through deeper cuts, I see its pit-spoil flesh,

coal-dark in each wound. Each entrance is closed by growth. I haul
to the top of one of its mounds to see the shape of what is left. Up this high,

I see its blurred labyrinth. Skedaddling down, I cheat my way into its wheels,
let its tangled alleys choose my coiled path, lead me round its dizzy veins.

The artist built its mystery of rings, raised its puzzle from soil so we could
lose ourselves; be found again. It is my bloom and bracken oubliette —

I wish I had come when it was sharp and I didn't mind being forgotten.
It is gentled after the grind of many years. Its claim is looser upon this Earth,

as is mine. *Erode, erode*. The wind curls a song through the maze's heart.
How I love you, secret hallow of strangely broken ground.

Notes

When I was sent to Coventry for real: 'Sent to Coventry' is a term used to deliberately ostracise someone; to refuse to communicate with someone, or act as if a person does not exist in order to inflict distress on another person.

The Effects of Rage: "Rage, rage against the dying of the light" – 'Do not go gentle into that good night', Dylan Thomas. "Cruel, with fury" - *Isaiah* 13:9. "we're not in Kansas anymore" – Dorothy Gale, *The Wizard of Oz*, film, 1939. "my eyes, my shoes. My rage" – 'Walking Around', Pablo Neruda.

The Unknown Women: The Unknown Women are two stone effigies dating from the early 14th century. Italic sections are lines of a prayer from a Book of Hours, 1514 which is displayed with the effigies.

At The Laing: *The Breton Shepherdess* by Paul Gaugin, 1886. *Jason in Hyde Park* by Mike Silva, 2020. *Isabella and the Pot of Basil* by William Holman Hunt, 1867

Thwarted Belongingness   (A Pandemic Funeral): Thwarted Belongingness is used as part of a suicidality assessment (SGQ-ASC) tool for people with autism. Thwarted Belongingness is a mental state that worsens when the need for connectedness and belonging is not met. Studies have shown that autistic people are at more risk of suicidal thoughts compared to people without autism. (Cassidy, S.A., Bradley, L., Cogger-Ward, H. et al. Development and validation of the suicidal behaviors questionnaire – autism spectrum conditions in a community sample of autistic, possibly autistic and non-autistic adults. Molecular Autism 12, 46 (2021). https://doi.org/10.1186/s13229-021-00449-3)

metapoem / iteration (Dickinson, 568) Liquor: "the black liquor with which men write" - Dr. Samuel Johnson

Pantoum to Maud's Absolutely Brilliant Door: Maud Lewis (1901-1970) was a Canadian folk artist. She lived her life in poverty and painted continuously, despite worsening rheumatoid arthritis, which in particular, affected her hands. She lived with her husband, Everett, in a tiny, one-room wooden home which she painted with her beautiful designs.

I hadn't heard poetry read out loud before, or talked about as if it was a Real & Important Thing until a brilliant teacher made it so: "I was much too far out all my life /And not waving but drowning", 'Not Waving but Drowning', by Stevie Smith "The water breathed on. / The water mixed with chrism and with oil", 'Clearances', by Seamus Heaney.

On Writing an Acceptance to the Self: *"right down and write myself a letter"* taken from the song, 'I'm Gonna Sit Right Down and Write Myself a Letter', written by Joe Young/Fred Ahlert, 1935.

Interoception: "Interoception is an internal sensory system in which the physical and emotional states of the person are consciously or unconsciously noticed, recognised and responded to. Interoception skills are required for a range of basic and more advanced functions, such as knowing when to go to the toilet or being aware that you are becoming angry or upset...interoception can slow down or even stop for autistic people...Many autistic people experience trauma, and this may halt or lower their interoceptive awareness." (National Autistic Society).

Me and the Goldsworthy, Alone: The Leadgate Maze is an earthwork creation designed by Andy Goldsworthy in a small ex-mining village in County Durham. It was built in 1989 on the site of the old Eden Colliery. It is rarely visited and almost unknown today and is much worn and overgrown. His artworks are designed to do no harm to the environment.

Note on How & Why I Invented the Ocular Map:

The page becomes the place I sing myself.   The space becomes
the place where I can live,

"[w]here the paper and body and ink and breath exist..." (White, 2015)

Poems are what our soul wants them to be. We offer them our tongues,
scribe them in blood.

I speak my creativity like a Babel Tower.   Learn the dialects
of space.   Know the metacommunication of the page.
Call across genres.   Find the nothing.   Make my mark.

Can words be viewed like art? Do they, in order to exist,
have to be read?

How does it feel to challenge an established / expected / accepted way
of reading? I investigated the grouping of areas of text
into their own separate entities, almost as if
they were mini-poems,   or poems within a poem.

Perhaps it seemed easier to read where my eye fell, rather than attempt
to scan the whole page at once.   The poem was:

>   "...disrupting the normal conventions of page layout as
>   to call into question the possibility of sequential reading,
>   top to bottom and left to right... [I found that I was absorbed
>   into] a tracing of shape, pattern and verbal links across and
>   around the page...[a] disruption of linearity."
>   (Knowles, K et al., 2012, p.6)

What if you did not start left and go right, left, right, along and down?
What happens to the words? What if we read them, but not in the
traditional order?

What if textual, visual and spatial elements adopt the role of

"...guiding the eye and the mind of the reader...[toward]
more subtle units of meaning...challenging the notion that...
type reigns supreme?"

(Knowles, K et al., 2012, pp. 2, 3)

What if, instead of waiting for 'happy accidents' on the page,
I directed my poem and established this way of writing as a form
in its own right?

Here was language freed from stricture.
Here was word feral, word roaming at will, word free.

There is a John Cage quote, concerning language demilitarisation:

"...what was interesting me was making English less
understandable. Because when it's understandable, well,
people control one another, and poetry disappears..."

(Sturm, 2014)

Removed from any typical structure, the words I used
were revealed to me in new, fascinating arrangements, as if I had
come to them as a stranger, and not their original author.

I let my eyes fall wherever they wished. I invite the reader to view them in
any way they wish. Wrong and right are no dictats here.

These are no happy accidents — instead, think of them as
controlled accidents, deliberate accidents; a legitimate altering
of a poem's destiny.

There is an undeniable inheritance connecting concrete poetry,
abstract art and the function of white space in poetry / creative
writing. I was fascinated by Mary Ellen Solt and the potential she
saw for:

"...enlarging [a poem's] possibilities for expression
and communication."

(Solt (ed.), 1971, p.7)

The particular book this quote came from (*Concrete Poetry: A World View*) was published the year I was born — please don't laugh when I say I can't help postulating that there is something mystical, serendipitous and fated interred within that particular fact.

To commemorate this amazing permutation, Solt and her work became the content of my first attempt at wielding my invented form, the Ocular Map.

Sources:

Knowles, K, Schaffer, A, Weger, U & Roberts, M. *Reading Space in Visual Poetry: New Cognitive Perspectives. Writing Technologies, vol. 4* (2012), 75-106 ISSN 1754-9035. https://www.ntu.ac.uk/__data/assets/pdf_file/0029/827093/Kim-Knowles,-Anna-Schaffner,-Ulrich-Weger,-Andrew-Roberts-Reading-Space-in-Visual-Poetry-New-Cognitive-Perspective.pdf.

Solt, Mary Ellen, Edited by. *Concrete Poetry: A World View*. Indiana University Press, Bloomington, London, 1970.

Solt, Mary Ellen. 'Flowers in Concrete I'. *Poetry Magazine,* March 1966. https://www.poetryfoundation.org/poetrymagazine/browse?volume=107&issue=6&page=32.

Sturm, Sean. *JOHN CAGE ON THE DEMILITARIZATION OF LANGUAGE. TE IPU PAKORE: THE BROKEN VESSEL,* 11th June, 2014. https://seansturm.wordpress.com/2014/06/11/john-cage-on-the-demilitarization-of-language/.

White, Orlando. 'Functional White: Crafting Space & Silence'. *Poetry Foundation,* 3rd November, 2015. https://www.poetryfoundation.org/harriet-books/2015/11/functional-white-crafting-sp ace-silence.

Acknowledgements

'This poem must be about' first published on *Hotazel Review*. 'Translation / Acts' first published on *Poetry Wales* website. 'When I was sent to Coventry for real' was awarded 3rd prize in the 2023 Poets, Prattlers and Pandemonialists poetry competition. 'Revelations 01/01/2022' first published on *The Friday Poem*. 'Augury' first published on *Black Iris*. 'when I balanced who I am upon the turning of a book' awarded 2nd prize in the 2022 Spectrum poetry competition and published by Renaud Press in the competition anthology. 'Epiphany / Turning 50' first published on *Northern Gravy*. 'The National Trust Cannot Charge You To Come In' first published in *Poetry London*. 'On Hawkburn Head' made the final 3 out of 600 in the 2022 Shepton Mallet Poetry Competition. 'Aisling to Dún a Rí' first published in *14 Magazine*. 'The Effects of Rage' longlisted in the Gloucester Poetry Society Poetry Competition, 2023. 'Mother Crow, Mother Bee, Mother Stone, Mother Sky' longlisted in the 2022 National Poetry Competition, shortlisted in the *Aesthetica* Creative Writing Award 2023. 'where tulips fade and tongues are put to rest' first published in *Strix*. 'Taraxacum' awarded 1st place in the 2023 Shepton Mallet Poetry Competition. 'An Evanescent Garden' first published on *Northern Gravy*. 'The Women who are Dead' first published in *Crannog*. 'I was a woman today' first published on *Culture Matters*. 'Marsh Angels' awarded 1st prize in the 2023 Edward Thomas Fellowship poetry competition. 'Ceridwen' first published in *Poetry Wales*. 'I'm afraid of the ghost of Egas Moniz' shortlisted in the 2021 Live Canon poetry competition and published in the competition anthology. 'I see you | hold the secrets of myself' highly commended in the 2021 Yorkmix poetry competition. 'Pantoum to Maud's Absolutely Brilliant Door' first published in *Poetry Wales*. 'Elizabeth's Fish' awarded 1st prize in the 2023 *Dark Winter Literary Magazine* poetry competition. 'I am Road, I am Mother, I am a Better Person Now, I am Failed' first published on *Culture Matters*. 'Eliza   save yourself from Higgins   run' highly commended in the 2022 Red Shed poetry competition. 'Hare cannot stop looking at a photograph of E.R. Fightmaster in a meadow' awarded 1st place in the 2021 Waltham Forest poetry competition.

'Ocular Map   Three Interpretations' first published in *Poetry Wales* if I was all the tiny horses ...clung' highly commended in the 2021 Cheltenham Festival Wildfire Words poetry competition. 'Afterwinter' first published in *Lighthouse Literary Journal.* 'When Pauline Sings Big River' first published in *Poetry Wales.* 'To the Kilburn Horse, seen from the Leeds to Newcastle train' longlisted in the 2022 National Poetry Competition, runner up in the 2023 Live Canon Poetry Competition.